W9-ASO-862

Martin Luther King, Jr.

Man of Peace

Patricia and Fredrick McKissack

Illustrated by Ned O.

❖ *Great African Americans Series* ❖

ENSLOW PUBLISHERS, INC.

44 Fadem Road
Box 699
Springfield, N.J. 07081
U.S.A.

P.O. Box 38
Aldershot
Hants GU12 6BP
U.K.

For Ruth Nell and Richard Petway

Library of Congress Cataloging-in-Publication Data

McKissack, Pat, 1944-
    Martin Luther King, Jr.: man of peace / Patricia & Fredrick McKissack.
        p. cm — (Great African-Americans series)
    Includes index.
    Summary: Simple text and illustrations describe the life and accomplishments of the revered civil rights worker.
    ISBN 0-89490-302-0
    1. King, Martin Luther, Jr., 1929-1968—Juvenile literature. 2. Afro-Americans—Biography—Juvenile literature. 3. Baptists—United States—Clergy—Biography—Juvenile literature. 4. Civil rights workers—United States—Biography—Juvenile literature [1. King, Martin Luther, Jr. 1929-1968. 2. Civil rights workers. 3. Clergy. 4. Afro-Americans—Biography.]
  I. McKissack, Fredrick. II. Title III. Series.
E185.97.K5M363 1991
323'.092—dc20
[B]
[92]   90-19156
                                        CIP
                                        AC

Printed in the United States of America

10 9 8 7 6 5

Photo credits: Jim Goodwyn, Montgomery, Alabama, p. 14; John F. Kennedy Library, pp. 21, 23; Lyndon Baines Johnson Library, pp. 26, 27; National Archives, p. 12; Southern Christian Leadership Conference, pp. 4, 20, 28; United Nations, p. 24; UPI/Bettmann Newsphotos, pp. 15, 22.

Illustration Credits: Ned O., pp. 6, 7, 8, 10, 16, 18.

Cover Illustration: Ned O.

Contents

Rev. Dr. Martin Luther King, Jr.
Born: January 15, 1929, Atlanta, Georgia.
Died: April 4, 1968, Memphis, Tennessee.

1

Because You Are Colored

Martin Luther King, Jr. grew up in a big, brick house on Auburn Avenue in Atlanta, Georgia.

Martin Luther King, Sr. was a Baptist **preacher***. Everybody called him Daddy King. He was a strong, proud man, who taught his children to be proud also. Mrs.

---

* Words in **bold type** are explained in *Words to Know* on page 30.

King was "Mother Dear" to her three children.

Young Martin's family called him M.L. But his friends called him "Tweed," because he wore **tweed** suits. His friends also called him "Will Shoot," because whenever the basketball was passed to him, he would shoot it.

There was also a serious side to Martin. He questioned **segregation**. Segregation

meant that black people were treated differently than other people. Why did they have to ride on the back seat of buses? Use separate public bathrooms? And drink from different water fountains? He was told: *because you are* **colored**!

That's the way things were in the South when Martin was growing up. Once, Martin made a speech. He won first place.

He and his teacher rode the bus home. The bus filled up. So, the driver told the black riders they had to give their seats to white passengers. When Martin asked why, he was told: *because you are colored!*

Even though Martin Luther King, Jr. was young, he felt segregation was not a good way for Americans to live. Black and white people should have the same rights.

2

Morehouse and More . . .

Martin still had fun growing up. He loved a good **soul-food** meal prepared by his grandmother. He did so well in school, he graduated from high school at the age of fifteen. In the fall of 1944, he entered Morehouse College in Atlanta.

What was Martin going to be? Daddy King said he should be a preacher. Martin wasn't so sure about that. He was still very young. He had a lot of questions about people, God, and what he would do in life.

A very important person in his life during that time was Dr. Benjamin Mays, the **president** of Morehouse. Dr. Mays was a very good friend and helped Martin look for his own answers.

By the time he finished Morehouse in the class of 1948, Martin knew he wanted to be a preacher. So, he went to Crozer

Theological **Seminary** in Chester, Pennsylvania.

At Crozer, Martin read about Mohandas Gandhi who helped India gain freedom from England—peacefully. Martin also read the writings of Henry David Thoreau, who said an unfair law should not be obeyed. Martin studied the words of Jesus and other holy leaders. His studies helped him find ways to fight **prejudice** peacefully.

There was racial prejudice in the North as well as the South. But, whenever it came up, Martin handled it peacefully. His classmates looked up to him, and even his enemies became his friends.

Love and peace were becoming very important words in Martin Luther King, Jr.'s life.

In 1958 Dr. King wrote *Stride Toward Freedom*. It was his first book. While at a book store in New York, a woman tried to kill him. His life was saved.

3

Peaceful Protest

After finishing Crozer Seminary in 1951, Martin went to Boston University. While living in Boston, Martin met Coretta Scott from Alabama. She was studying music at a school in Boston.

After their first date, Martin asked Coretta to marry him. She thought he was joking, but he wasn't. "She was everything I wanted in a wife," he told his best friend. And on June 18, 1953, Martin and Coretta were married.

Martin got his advanced degree in **theology** and Coretta finished her studies, too. Then the Kings had to decide where they would live. A church in the South had asked Dr. King to come there. Mrs. King wanted to stay in the North at first. The South was still very segregated. But at

Martin and Coretta named one of their sons Dexter to honor their first church—Dexter Avenue Baptist Church. The King's other children are Yolanda, Martin, Jr., and Bernice.

last, they decided to go back "down home."

In December 1954, Reverend Dr. Martin Luther King, Jr. preached his first sermon as the pastor of Dexter Avenue Baptist Church in Montgomery, Alabama.

A year passed. It was December 1, 1955. Rosa Parks got off from work and boarded a public bus. The bus filled. She

King was a powerful speaker. People listened when he spoke. Even when he was arrested in Montgomery, Dr. King still said, "We will not turn to violence."

was asked to give her seat to a white passenger. Mrs. Parks refused. At that time, it was against the law for Mrs. Parks to refuse to give up her seat to a white person when the bus was crowded. So she was taken to the police station.

Black leaders in Montgomery called a meeting that evening at Dr. King's church. It was decided that a bus strike might help to change the unfair laws. Dr. King was asked to be the leader. He said he would, but only if the people taking part in the bus strike were peaceful.

For months and months, black people of Montgomery didn't ride public buses. One year later, the bus company agreed to let people, black and white, sit where they wanted.

4

To the Mountaintop

After the Montgomery Bus strike, Dr. King started the Southern Christian Leadership Conference (SCLC). He moved his family to Atlanta. Daddy King was very happy to have his son and family home again.

The South was changing. Young people were helping it happen. **Students** at North Carolina A&T University held a peaceful **sit-in** at segregated lunch counters.

Black and white students were working

together to make America a better place.
Black and white students formed a group
under the SCLC known as Student
Non-Violent Coordinating Committee, or
SNCC (pronounced SNICK). The group
held **sit-ins** and peaceful **protests** all over
the country. Americans were taking a
stand against segregation—even if it

In the summer of 1961, whites and blacks rode buses
together from one southern city to another. They were
called "Freedom Riders."

meant they were beaten or put in jail. Dr. King was jailed many times, too. But he always said to stay peaceful.

In 1963 two well-known leaders, A. Philip Randolph and Bayard Rustin, planned a march on Washington for jobs and freedom. Other black leaders were asked to take part.

A. Philip Randolph (second from left) was an important civil rights leader. It was his idea to hold the March on Washington, August 28, 1963. He introduced Rev. King, who was the last speaker on the program.

On a hot August morning in 1963, over 250,000 people came to Washington, D.C. to the largest **demonstration** for rights ever held in this country! People came from all over the world in airplanes, trains, buses, and cars. Some walked, and some were carried. The large crowd was orderly

Dr. King's "I Have a Dream" speech is remembered most often. He hoped that one day his four children would not be "judged by the color of their skin . . ."

and peaceful. They sang songs. A favorite was called "We Shall Overcome."

Many people gave speeches that day. It was the end of a long day. There was one more speaker. Martin Luther King, Jr.

He talked about having a dream where Americans lived in peace and friendship. "Let Freedom ring," he said. And one day, he hoped all Americans might sing, "Free at last, free at last . . ."

After the March on Washington, Dr. King and other civil rights leaders met with President John F. Kennedy in the White House. The president promised to work for civil rights, too.

Dr. Ralph Bunche won the Nobel Peace Prize in 1950. Here, Dr. Bunche greets Dr. and Mrs. King at the United Nations.

5

We Shall Overcome

For his work, Dr. King was given the **Nobel Peace Prize** in 1964. He was the second African American to win this high honor.

President John F. Kennedy had pushed for laws that would protect the rights of all races. But he had been killed on November 22, 1963. President Lyndon B. Johnson wanted to work for equal rights, too. Dr. King was at the White House the

day President Johnson signed the Voting
Rights Act on August 6, 1965.

Dr. King believed in peace. Some
people didn't. They beat his followers.
Churches were burned. Dogs and water
hoses were turned on peaceful marchers.
People were put in jail. Some were even

Dr. King and others watch as President Lyndon B.
Johnson signs the Voting Rights Act in August 1965. Five
days later a riot began in Watts (Los Angeles), California.
Dr. King was against all violence—including the war in
Vietnam.

killed. Many times people said they wanted to kill Dr. King.

Workers in Memphis, Tennessee asked him to help them plan a peaceful march. Dr. King went to Memphis.

The march ended in **violence**. This bothered Dr. King very much. He wanted

Robert Kennedy (right) was President Kennedy's brother. He ran for president, too, in 1968. But, Robert Kennedy was killed June 6, 1968. It was a very sad time.

to hold another march. So he returned to Memphis.

He stayed at the Lorraine Motel. On April 4, 1968, Martin Luther King, Jr. was killed by James Earl Ray. Ray is serving a life sentence in a Tennessee state prison.

Dr. King is dead, but his dream lives on. He is a world hero who is loved by all people who dream and work for peace and freedom.

Mrs. Coretta King began the Center for **Non-Violent** Social Change, in Atlanta. People come from all over the world to study Dr. King's life, writings, and peaceful demonstrations.

Today the birthday of Martin Luther King, Jr. is a holiday. On the third Monday in January we honor his work and his dream. If his dream is remembered, then one day we might live together in peace.

fri

Words to Know

colored—An outdated name for African Americans.

demonstration—A public showing of feelings for or against an issue.

Nobel Peace Prize—A special honor given to a person who works for peace in the world. It is named after the man who left money in his will to start the prize.

non-violent (non-VY-uh-lent)—Without violence, peaceful.

preacher—A teacher of religion.

prejudice (PREJ-uh-dis)—Dislike of people, places, or things without a good reason.

president—Leader of a country or group.

segregation (seg-ruh-GAY-shun)—The separation of people based on race, religion, age, sex, or some other reason.

seminary—A school where religion is studied.

sit-ins—A kind of demonstration; they began as black and white people sat at lunch counters until they were served. Later, sit-ins were used to object to different things, like war, poverty, and world hunger.

soul-food—Food prepared in much the same way as African Americans did during the time of slavery.

students—People who attend a school.

theology (thee-AHL-uh-gee)—The study of religion.

tweed—A warm, heavy material made of different colors of wool woven together.

violence (VY-uh-lents)—Acts that hurt or destroy people, places, animals, and other things.

INDEX